Skills On Studying

HELP IS ON THE WAY FOR:

Listening Skills

Written by Marilyn Berry
Pictures by Bartholomew

CHILDRENS PRESS ®
CHICAGO

Childrens Press
School and Library Edition
ISBN 0-516-03285-2

Executive Producer: Marilyn Berry
Editor: Theresa Tinkle
Consultants: Terie Snyder and Eleanor Villalpando
Design and Art Direction: Abigail Johnston
Typesetting: Curt Chelin

So you need to learn some **listening skills!**

Hang on! Help is on the way!

If you are having a hard time
- hearing what people say,
- understanding what people say,
- responding to what people say, or
- remembering what people say...

...you are not alone!

Just in case you're wondering...

...why don't we start at the beginning?

What Does It Mean To Listen?

To listen means to pay attention in order to hear. There are two types of listening: *passive* listening and *active* listening.

Passive listening is a relaxed activity that requires little effort or thought. An example of passive listening is listening to background music.

Active listening is an activity that requires more effort and thought. An example of active listening is listening to someone speak. When you listen to someone speak, you usually try to *hear* and *understand* what the person is saying.

Why Are Listening Skills Important?

Listening skills are tools that can help you to hear and understand what a person is saying. Good listening skills will help you
- hear more accurately,
- understand more of what you hear,
- respond appropriately to what you hear, and
- remember more of what you hear.

Listening is an important part of communication. The better your listening skills, the better you will communicate. Listening is also an important part of learning. The better your listening skills, the more you will learn. Listening skills can be easy to learn if you take it one step at a time.

Steps To Successful Listening

There are five simple steps you can follow that will help you become a successful listener:

- Eliminate the obstacles.
- Listen with your ears.
- Listen with your eyes.
- Listen with your mind.
- Respond to the message.

Step One: Eliminate The Obstacles

The first step to successful listening is to get rid of any obstacles that could keep you from hearing what the speaker is saying. Here are some common obstacles to look for:

Poor Reception
If you can't hear clearly, you can't listen. Make sure you are close enough to the speaker and that the speaker talks loudly and clearly enough for you to hear what is being said.

Outside Distractions

It is hard to listen to someone when there are things around you that take your attention away from the speaker. So that you can give the speaker your full attention, you may need to

- find a place without distractions,
- eliminate the distractions, or
- learn to ignore the distractions and focus on what is being said.

Inside Distractions

It is also hard to listen to someone when you have other thoughts on your mind. To give the speaker your full attention, you may need to

- put the other thoughts out of your mind and try to focus on what the speaker is saying, or
- suggest that the conversation take place at another time.

Step Two: Listen With Your Ears

The second step to successful listening is to listen carefully to *what* the speaker is saying and *how* he or she is saying it. You will need to listen carefully to the speaker's
- words and
- tone of voice.

The Speaker's Words

When someone is talking to you, it is important to listen carefully to his or her choice of words. You need to

- make sure you have heard the words correctly and
- listen to the words in the context of the message. Words can take on different meanings depending on how the speaker uses them.

The Speaker's Tone of Voice

When a person is talking to you, it is also important to notice his or her tone of voice. *How* a speaker says something can change the meaning of what he or she is saying. A person's tone of voice can tell you

- how the person feels about the subject and
- whether the person is serious or joking.

Step Three: Listening With Your Eyes

The third step to successful listening is to use your eyes to help you listen. When a person talks to you, he or she will most often use more than just words to communicate. Many times a person will use
• body language and
• visual aids
to get a point across.

Body Language

You will understand more of what a speaker is
saying if you watch what the person is doing as
he or she talks. You will want to watch the
person's

- facial expressions,
- posture, and
- gestures.

Visual Aids

Many times a speaker will use a visual aid to help make a point. You will understand more of what the speaker is saying if you will look closely at the visual aid as you listen to the person talk.

Step Four: Listen With Your Mind

The fourth step to successful listening is to use your mind to help you understand and evaluate what the speaker is saying. When a person talks to you, you need to
- clarify the message,
- interpret the message, and
- examine the message.

Clarify the Message

To clarify means to make clear. When you clarify what someone is saying, you make sure that you are hearing the speaker correctly. You can clarify the message by

- asking questions about the message and
- putting the message in your own words.

Interpret the Message

One meaning of the word *interpret* is *explain*. Once you are sure you have heard the message correctly, you may still need some further explanation. To make sure you completely understand, you may need to ask the speaker to interpret the message for you.

Examine the Message

Once you understand what the speaker is saying, you need to take a closer look at the message. You need to think about

- how you feel about the message,
- whether you agree or disagree with the message, and
- what further information you need or want to know about the message.

Step Five: Respond To The Message

The final step to successful listening is to choose an appropriate response. The speaker needs to know that you have been listening and that you understand what he or she has been saying. Appropriate responses might be

- facial expressions,
- gestures,
- single words,
- simple statements,
- questions,
- long detailed comments.

Learning to use the five steps for successful listening is not hard. However, it does take some concentration and practice. The more you practice these steps, the more automatic they will become for you. Soon you will be using these listening skills without even thinking about them.

Tips For Successful Listening In School

You are required to spend a large part of every school day listening to your teachers. The five steps to successful listening will make listening in school much easier. There are also several tips that can help you improve your listening in school:

- Come to school prepared.
- Always be ready to listen.
- Know what to listen for.
- Remember what you hear.

Come To School Prepared

Listening in school is more meaningful and takes less effort when you come to school prepared to listen. Here are three things you can do to help prepare yourself:

1. **Keep up with your homework.** Many times the topics your teacher discusses on one day are related to the topics discussed the day before. Keeping up with your homework will give you some background for the new information that is being presented.

2. **Get some background information.** The more you know about a topic, the easier it is to listen to someone talk about it. If possible, try to get some background information on a topic *before* your teacher talks about it in class. Find out which topic your teacher plans to discuss the following day. Then either read a chapter ahead in your textbook or look up the topic in an encyclopedia.

3. **Make up a list of questions.** It is usually more interesting to listen to someone talk about a topic when you are curious about it. When you find out the topic your teacher will be discussing, write down a few questions that come to mind. As your teacher talks, try to listen for the answers.

Be Ready To Listen

An important tip for listening in school is to try always to be alert and ready to listen. You can make sure you are ready if you follow four simple rules:

1. **Choose a good seat.** Try to sit in a place where you can clearly see and hear the teacher. Remember also to choose a spot that is free from distractions.

2. **Don't talk or pass notes.** When you take time out from your listening to talk to a friend or write a friend a note, you could be missing some important information. Save your talking and note-passing for recess and lunch breaks. During class time try to keep your eyes and ears tuned in to the teacher.

3. **Don't doodle or daydream.** Doodling and daydreaming are both fun activities. However, when you do them in class, your attention is not where it needs to be. While you are in class, give the teacher and your schoolwork your full attention. Then set aside some time after school to doodle and daydream.

4. **Don't make up homework in class.** When you get behind in a subject, don't make up the work in another class. You will only fall further behind. If you listen carefully and pay attention during each class, you will have a better chance of keeping up with your work.

Know What To Listen For

Before your teacher shares information with the class, he or she has spent time making an outline of what to say. Sometimes your teacher will share the outline with the class so you can follow along. Your teacher might put the outline on the chalkboard or on a study sheet. This outline will give you a clue of what to listen for.

At other times you will be expected to find the outline on your own. As your teacher explains the topic to the class, you will be looking for two types of information:

1. The main ideas.
2. The supporting details.

This information is not hard to recognize when you know what to listen for.

The Main Ideas

When your teacher presents new information to your class, one of your goals is to pick out the most important points. The most important points are the *main ideas* of the talk. Most often these points are plainly stated in the introduction or summary of the talk. However, sometimes they are only suggested. You can find a main idea by asking yourself:

If you listen carefully, the teacher will sometimes give you clues that will help you find the main ideas. Listen for phrases such as these:

- "My first point is..."
- "This is important..."
- "You should know..."
- "Be sure to remember..."
- "Next, we'll talk about..."

Main ideas are sometimes repeated throughout the talk.

The Supporting Details

Supporting details are pieces of information that further explain the main ideas. Supporting details may include

- examples and stories,
- descriptions,
- definitions,
- facts,
- quotations, or
- questions.

If you listen carefully, the teacher will sometimes give you clues that will help you find the supporting details. Listen for key phrases such as these:

- "For example..."
- "The reasons for..."
- "The causes of..."
- "That reminds me of a story..."

Remember What You Hear

Information you hear in school is usually information you will need to remember. Here are three things that can help you remember what you hear in class:

1. Repeat the information.
2. Write down the information.
3. Use a tape recorder.

Repeat the Information

It is easier to remember important information if you hear it more than once. You can accomplish this by repeating the information to yourself.

- As soon as your teacher makes an important point, repeat the point in your mind.
- Sometime later that day, try to remember the important points and repeat them aloud.

Write Down the Information

It is also easier to remember important information that you hear if you write it down. As your teacher talks, write down the main ideas and their supporting details. Then read through your notes at a later time.

Use a Tape Recorder
A tape recorder can be a valuable listening aid. You may use it in class and record your teacher's talks. Later you will have more time to go over the talks and find the main ideas and supporting details. You may also read your notes into a recorder and listen to them over and over.

Some Final Notes

If you have a hard time listening in school, try setting up a reward system for yourself. It will be easier to listen in school if you have something to look forward to.

If you have trouble listening, you may have problems with your hearing. Ask your school nurse to check your hearing if you have any of these symptoms:

- There is a ringing in your ears.
- You often ask people to repeat what they say.
- You often misunderstand what people say.
- Things sound muffled.

WARNING!

If you follow the suggestions in this book, you will probably become a better listener and...

...you may also become a better student!

THE END

About the Author
Marilyn Berry has a master's degree in education with a specialization in reading. She is on staff as a creator of supplementary materials at Living Skills Press. Marilyn and her husband Steve Patterson have two sons, John and Brent.

001.54 Berry, Marilyn
B
    Help is on the way
    for: listening
    skills

$13.2

001.54 Berry, Marilyn
B
    Help is on the way
    for: listening
    skills

$13.27

DATE	BORROWER'S NAME	
1-7-92	Ada n C.	T-6
2-16-93	Monica. a	27